WILD TURKEYS

Meryl Magby

PowerKiDS press
New York

For Noel Bohl-Fabian

Published in 2014 by The Rosen Publishing Group, Inc.
29 East 21st Street, New York, NY 10010

First Edition

Editor: Amelie von Zumbusch
Book Design: Ashley Drago
Layout Design: Colleen Bialecki

Photo Credits: Cover, p. 1 AlenKadr/Shutterstock.com; p. 5 KennStilger47/Shutterstock.com; p. 6 Zipp Jim/Photo Researchers/Getty Images; p. 7 Tom Reichner/Shutterstock.com; p. 8 Jeff Banke/Shutterstock.com; pp. 9 (top), 10, 19 (bottom) iStockphoto/Thinkstock; p. 9 (bottom) Melinda Fawver/Shutterstock.com; p. 11 Tim Laman/National Geographic/Getty Images; pp. 12–13 Darell Gulin/Photographer's Choice/Getty Images; p. 15 Photodisc/Thinkstock; p. 16 Karl Maslowski/Photo Researchers/Getty Images; p. 17 Steve Maslowski/Visuals Unlimited/Getty Images; p. 19 Leonard Lee Rue III/Photo Researchers/Getty Images; p. 19 (top) Paul S. Wolf/Shutterstock.com; p. 20 Superstock/Getty Images; p. 21 Gerald A. DeBoer/Shutterstock.com; p. 22 Adam Jones/Photodisc/Getty Images.

Library of Congress Cataloging-in-Publication Data

Magby, Meryl.
 Wild turkeys / by Meryl Magby — First edition.
      pages cm. — (American animals)
 Includes index.
 ISBN 978-1-4777-0787-6 (library binding) — ISBN 978-1-4777-0946-7 (paperback) — ISBN 978-1-4777-0947-4 (6-pack)
 1. Wild turkey—Juvenile literature. I. Title.
 QL696.G27M336 2014
 598.6'45—dc23

                                          2012045396

Manufactured in the United States of America

CPSIA Compliance Information: Batch #S13PK6: For Further Information contact Rosen Publishing, New York, New York at 1-800-237-9932

Contents

Gobble, Gobble

Wild turkeys are large birds that are **native** to North America. They are the same **species** as the turkeys many Americans eat for Thanksgiving dinner. However, Thanksgiving turkeys are usually **domesticated**. This means they are raised by people. Wild turkeys are wild animals. They run free in forests and fields across the United States.

> Wild turkeys have mostly dark feathers that help them blend in with their surroundings. Domesticated turkeys tend to be white.

Wild turkeys are game birds. People hunt them for food and sport. They are related to other game birds such as grouse, pheasant, partridge, and quail. Wild turkeys are known for the "gobble, gobble" sound that males make. Males are also known for fanning out their long tail feathers.

Where Turkeys Live

When **settlers** came from Europe, they found wild turkeys in most of eastern and central North America. Today, wild turkeys have an even larger range. There are wild turkeys in every US state except for Alaska and in parts of Canada and Mexico.

Turkeys do not usually roost in the same tree every night.

Wild turkeys' natural habitats are woods and grassy fields. Turkeys need tall trees to **roost** in at night and to hide from **predators**. They find many of the foods they eat on the forest floor. Grassy fields give female turkeys a place to lay eggs. Young turkeys also find many insects to eat there.

This wild turkey is in a hardwood forest in Pennsylvania. Hardwood forests have trees that drop their leaves in the winter.

Gobblers and Hens

Gobblers tend to stand about 2.5 feet (0.7 m) tall.

Wild turkeys are large birds. Adult male turkeys, called gobblers or toms, can weigh between 10 and 25 pounds (5–11 kg). Female turkeys, called hens, are generally smaller. Hens weigh between 8 and 12 pounds (4–5 kg).

Gobblers have dark feathers on their bodies, as well as striped wing and tail feathers. The skin on their heads is usually blue or white. A flap of skin called a snood hangs over a gobbler's beak. Another flap, called a wattle, hangs from its chin. Gobblers also have long hairlike feathers on their chests, called beards. Pointy **spurs** grow out of their legs.

The skin on a gobbler's head is generally blue or white. However, it turns red when the gobbler is ready to fight or court females.

Hens have rust-colored feathers. The skin on their heads is blue-gray.

Scratching for Food

Wild turkeys find food to eat in the woods and fields where they live. Adult turkeys eat mostly plants. Turkeys eat greens, fruits, berries, seeds, grains, and nuts. Turkeys also eat insects such as beetles, grasshoppers, flies, and moths. Young turkeys spend a lot of time in grassy fields eating insects. This helps them grow big and strong.

Turkeys eat more of certain foods depending on the time of year. In the winter, they eat a lot of nuts, seeds, and grains from fields.

Turkeys find food by scratching at the ground with their feet. In the winter months, it can be harder for wild turkeys to find food. However, turkeys can dig through up to 6 inches (15 cm) of snow to look for food.

Wild Turkey Facts

1. Wild turkeys can run up to 12 miles per hour (19 km/h) and fly up to 55 miles per hour (86 km/h). They can also swim!

2. Although they do not gobble, turkey hens also make sounds. Their calls include yelps, clucks, and purrs.

3. Turkeys do not clean themselves in water. Instead, they take dust baths. This means they roll in the soil so that it can **absorb** oil from their skin and feathers.

4. Native Mexican peoples called Aztecs domesticated the wild turkey around 500 AD.

5. A small number of female turkeys have beards. However, that number is less than 1 percent.

6. Turkeys may try to attack their reflections in shiny objects, such as mirrors or pools of water.

7. Hens sometimes pretend they have a broken wing to lead predators away from their young.

The Pecking Order

Wild turkeys live in groups called flocks. The turkeys in a flock look for food together during the day and roost in trees at night. In a flock, turkeys have a **ranking**. Older, stronger birds generally rule over weaker, younger birds. The ranking is called a pecking order. This is because more **dominant** turkeys may peck at weaker turkeys.

> The pecking order in a wild turkey flock is very exact. Each bird has a ranking in relation to all the other birds in the flock.

Each spring, male turkeys try to attract female turkeys for **mating**. During this time, males fluff their feathers, fan their tails, strut, and gobble. Male turkeys also fight with each other over female turkeys. One male turkey may mate with many female turkeys during mating season.

Poults and Broods

After mating, hens leave their flocks to lay their eggs. They make their nests on the ground in the woods or a field. It takes each hen about two weeks to lay between 10 and 14 eggs. Then, the hens **incubate** their eggs for about 28 days until they hatch.

A mother's group of poults is known as a brood.

Hens take care of their young, called poults. The poults follow their mother everywhere. After they hatch, the hen leads them to a grassy field where they can eat insects. After about two weeks, the poults learn to fly. In late summer, hens and their young come together to form a flock again.

Newly hatched chicks are able to leave the nest within 24 hours to look for their first meal.

Turkey Predators

Wild turkeys are good fliers, unlike their domesticated relatives.

Wild turkeys have many predators, such as raccoons, coyotes, skunks, bobcats, snakes, owls, and foxes. Some predators steal turkey eggs. Others attack hens that are sitting on their eggs. Predators often go after poults because they are weaker and slower than adult turkeys. However, predators may also prey on adults, especially old or sick turkeys.

Wild turkeys have ways to keep safe from predators. Their good eyesight and hearing let them know if a predator is coming. Adult turkeys and older poults can fly up into tall trees, where some predators cannot reach them. Gobblers sometimes use their spurs to try to fight off predators.

Coyotes (left) and great horned owls (above) hunt both adult wild turkeys and wild turkey poults.

Turkeys and People

In the fall of 1621, the **Pilgrims** had a feast with Native Americans to celebrate their **harvest**. Many call this the first Thanksgiving. Historians disagree about whether the Pilgrims ate wild turkey at this feast. However, we know that wild turkeys were an important food for settlers.

This painting shows the first Thanksgiving. The Native Americans at the feast were Wampanoags.

Native Americans hunted turkeys for food, clothes, and tools long before the settlers arrived, too.

In time, more European settlers arrived. This meant that more people were hunting wild turkeys. The settlers cut down forests where turkeys lived for wood and to make room for farms. By the middle of the 19th century, wild turkeys were in danger of dying out.

Early American statesman Benjamin Franklin wrote in a letter to his daughter that the wild turkey would make a better national bird than the bald eagle.

The Turkey Comeback

By 1900, there were fewer than 30,000 wild turkeys in the United States. Today, there are more than 7 million wild turkeys in North America! How were wild turkeys saved?

After the Civil War, woodlands starting growing back because fewer people were farming. Then, in the 1950s, people started trapping wild turkeys and letting them go in places where the turkeys could find food and mate. Slowly, the wild turkey population grew again. Today, the wild turkey has made a true comeback.

This wild turkey is in Cades Cove, a part of Great Smoky Mountains National Park that is in Tennessee. National parks are a great place to see these birds.

Glossary

absorb (ub-SORB) To take in and hold on to something.

domesticated (duh-MES-tih-kayt-ed) Raised to live with people.

dominant (DAH-mih-nent) In charge.

harvest (HAR-vist) A season's gathered crops.

incubate (IN-kyoo-bayt) To keep eggs warm, usually at body temperature.

mating (MAY-ting) Coming together to make babies.

native (NAY-tiv) Born or grown in a certain place or country.

Pilgrims (PIL-grumz) The people who sailed from England to America in search of freedom to practice their own beliefs, starting in 1620.

predators (PREH-duh-terz) Animals that kill other animals for food.

ranking (RAN-king) The position someone or something has in a group.

roost (ROOST) To go to the place where one rests or sleeps.

settlers (SET-lerz) People who move to a new land to live.

species (SPEE-sheez) One kind of living thing. All people are one species.

spurs (SPERZ) Sharp parts that stick out from animals' bodies.

Index

Websites

Due to the changing nature of Internet links, PowerKids Press has developed an online list of websites related to the subject of this book. This site is updated regularly. Please use this link to access the list:
www.powerkidslinks.com/amer/turk/